A MAGICAL CHRISTMAS

15 YULETIDE SONGS ARRANGED BY PHILLIP KEVEREN

— PIANO LEVEL —
LATE ELEMENTARY

T0057208

ISBN 978-1-70514-019-2

Visit Hal Leonard Online at
www.halleonard.com

Visit Phillip at
www.phillipkeveren.com

Contact us:
Hal Leonard
7777 West Bluemound Road
Milwaukee, WI 53213
Email: info@halleonard.com

In Europe, contact:
Hal Leonard Europe Limited
42 Wigmore Street
Marylebone, London, W1U 2RN
Email: info@halleonardeurope.com

In Australia, contact:
Hal Leonard Australia Pty. Ltd.
4 Lentara Court
Cheltenham, Victoria, 3192 Australia
Email: info@halleonard.com.au

PREFACE

Learning to play the piano is exciting. One of the biggest rewards comes when the songs of Christmas are within reach. Melodies that make the season special are particularly pleasing when the music is coming from your own fingers!

This collection features some of the most famous Christmas songs. The tunes cover a lot of ground stylistically, from jazz-flavored standards like "The Christmas Song" to rock 'n' roll ditties like "Little St. Nick."

I hope you have a great time playing these arrangements!

Merry Christmas,

BIOGRAPHY

Phillip Keveren, a multi-talented keyboard artist and composer, has composed original works in a variety of genres from piano solo to symphonic orchestra. He gives frequent concerts and workshops for teachers and their students in the United States, Canada, Europe, and Asia. Mr. Keveren holds a B.M. in composition from California State University Northridge and a M.M. in composition from the University of Southern California.

CONTENTS

BELIEVE

from Warner Bros. Pictures' THE POLAR EXPRESS

Words and Music by GLEN BALLARD
and ALAN SILVESTRI
Arranged by Phillip Keveren

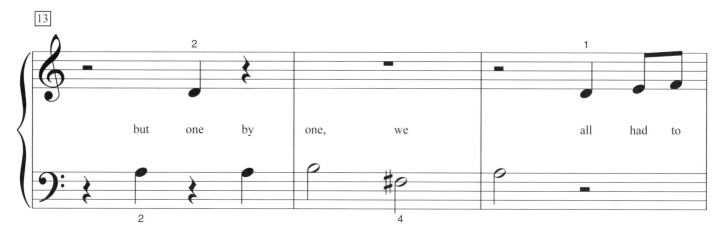

but one by one, we all had to

grow up. When it seems the mag - ic slipped a -

way, we find it all a - gain on Christ - mas

Day. Be - lieve in what your heart is say - ing,

hear the mel - o - dy that's play - ing. There's no time to waste, there's so

much to cel - e - brate. Be - lieve in what you feel in - side and

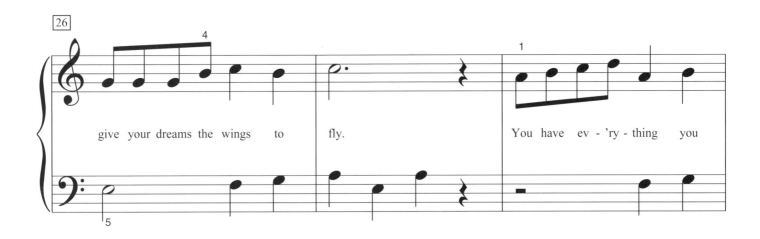

give your dreams the wings to fly. You have ev - 'ry - thing you

need, if you just be - lieve. _____

THE CHRISTMAS SONG
(Chestnuts Roasting on an Open Fire)

Music and Lyric by MEL TORMÉ
and ROBERT WELLS
Arranged by Phillip Keveren

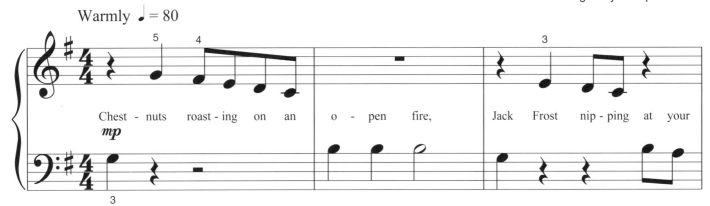

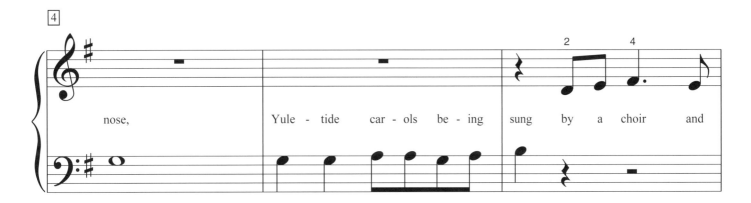

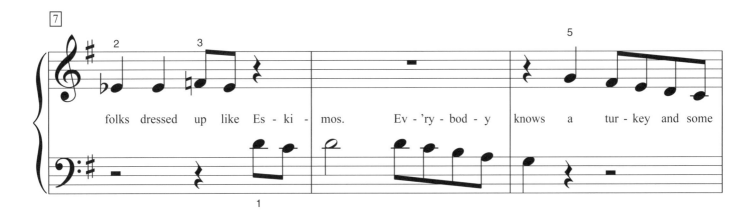

Ti - ny tots with their eyes all a - glow will find it hard to sleep to -

night. They know that San - ta's on his

p

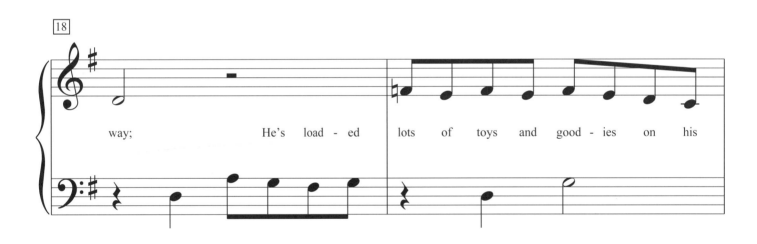

way; He's load - ed lots of toys and good - ies on his

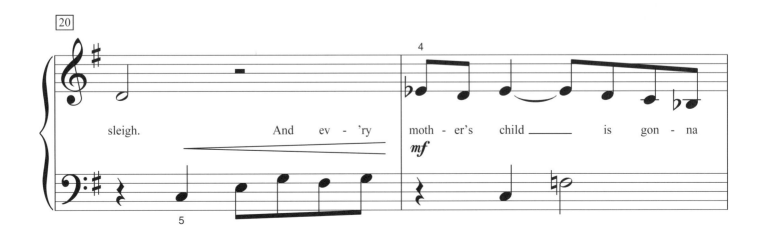

sleigh. And ev - 'ry moth - er's child _____ is gon - na

mf

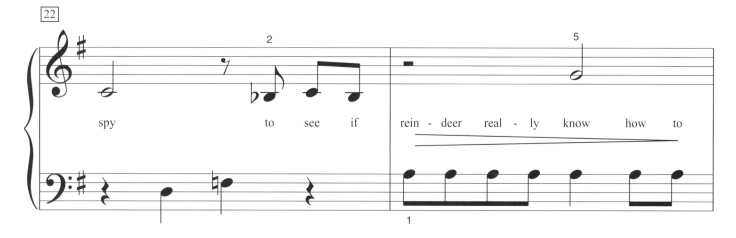

spy ... to see if reindeer really know how to

fly. And so, I'm offering this simple phrase to

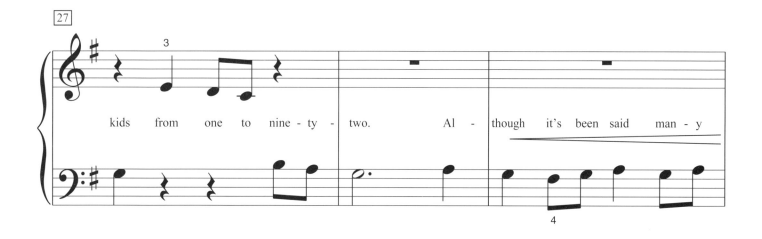

kids from one to ninety-two. Although it's been said many

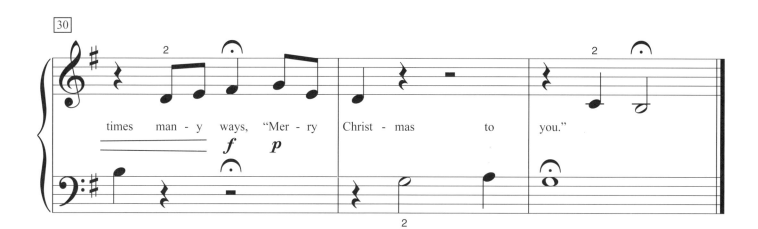

times many ways, "Merry Christmas to you."

THE CHIPMUNK SONG

Words and Music by ROSS BAGDASARIAN
Arranged by Phillip Keveren

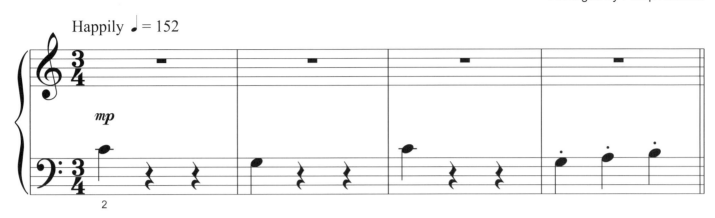

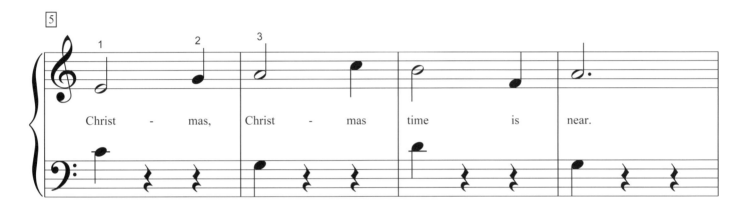

Christ - mas, Christ - mas time is near.

Time for toys and time for cheer.

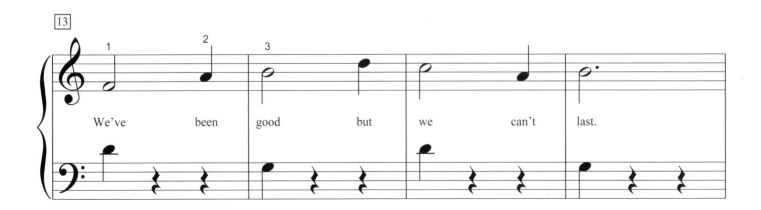

We've been good but we can't last.

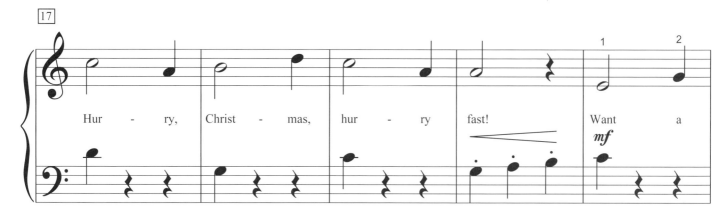

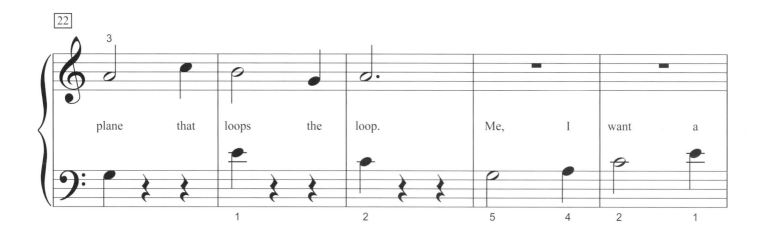

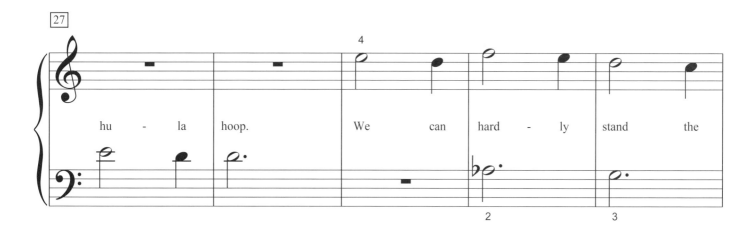

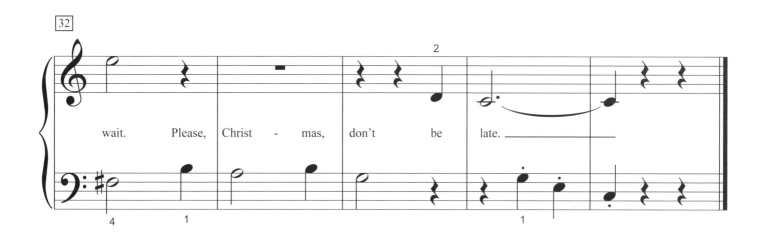

DO YOU WANT TO BUILD A SNOWMAN?

from FROZEN

Music and Lyrics by KRISTEN ANDERSON-LOPEZ
and ROBERT LOPEZ
Arranged by Phillip Keveren

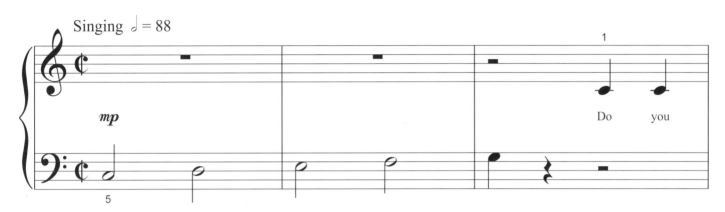

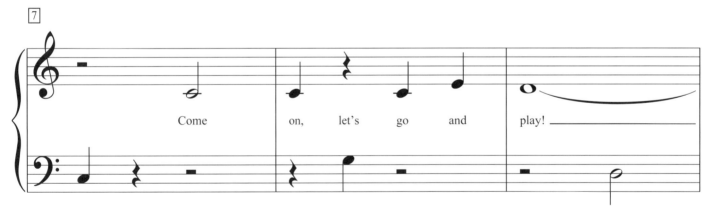

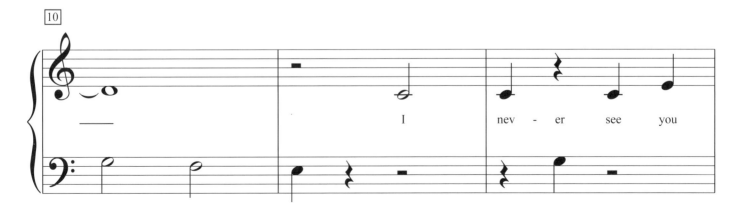

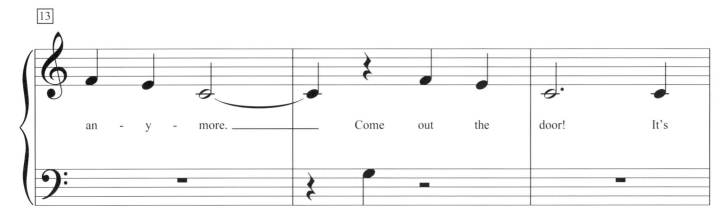

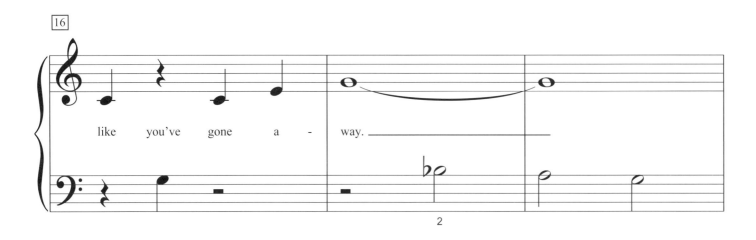

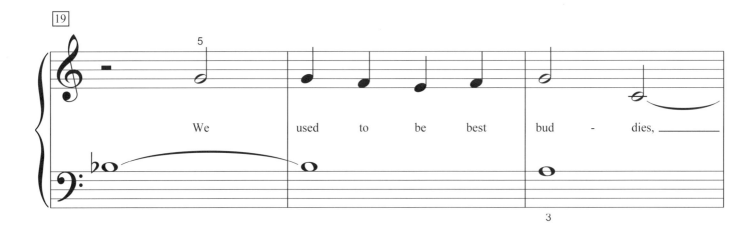

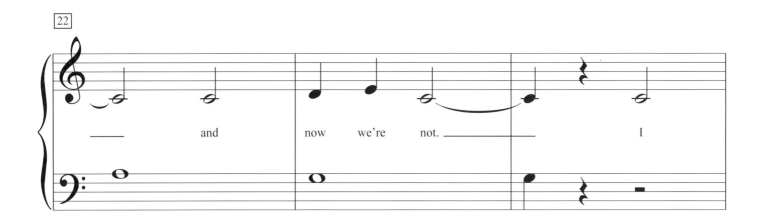

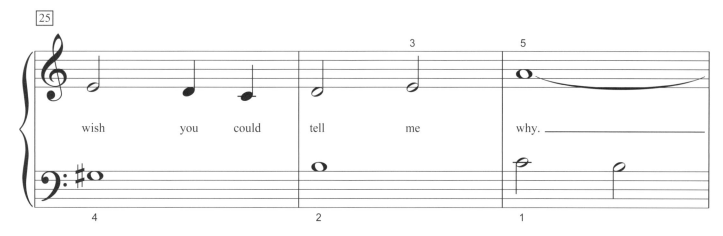

25

wish   you   could   tell   me   why. _____

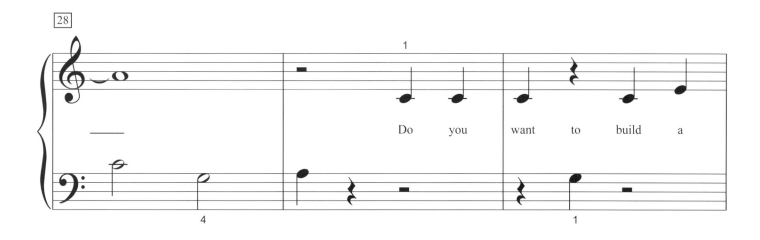

28

Do   you   want   to   build   a

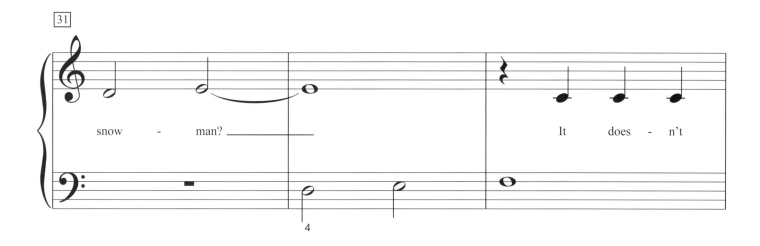

31

snow - man? _____   It   does - n't

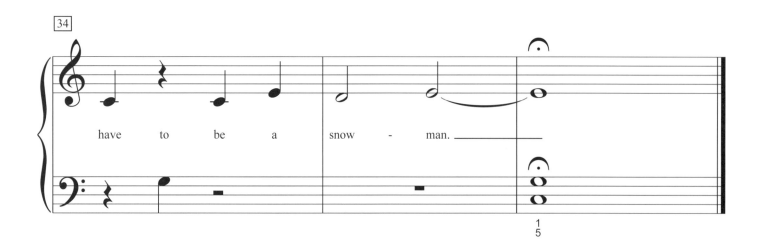

34

have   to   be   a   snow - man. _____

FROSTY THE SNOW MAN

Words and Music by STEVE NELSON
and JACK ROLLINS
Arranged by Phillip Keveren

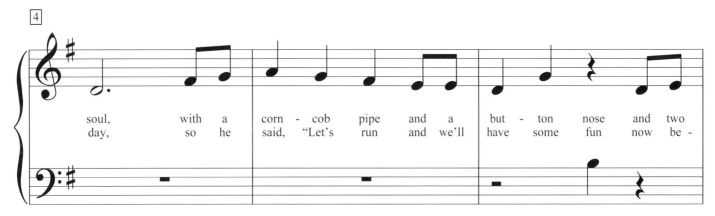

chil - dren know how he | came to life one | day. There | must have been some
round the square, say - in' | "Catch me if you | can." He | led them down the

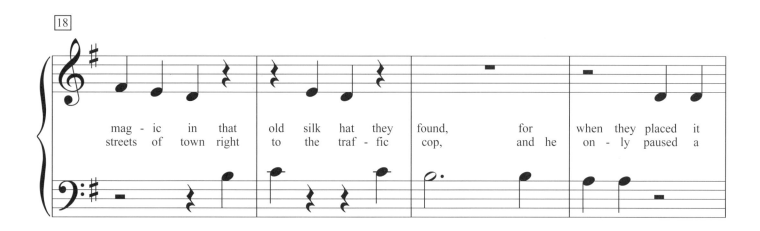

mag - ic in that | old silk hat they | found, for | when they placed it
streets of town right | to the traf - fic | cop, and he | on - ly paused a

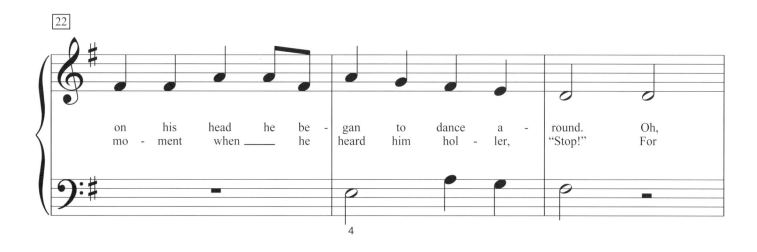

on his head he be - | gan to dance a - | round. Oh,
mo - ment when ___ he | heard him hol - ler, | "Stop!" For

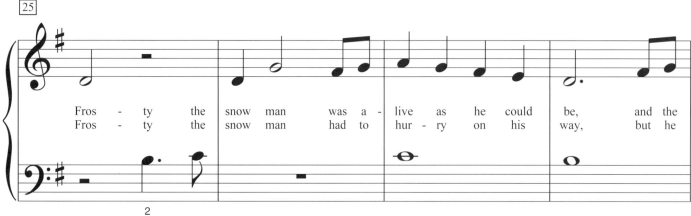

Fros - ty the snow man was a - | live as he could | be, and the
Fros - ty the snow man had to | hur - ry on his | way, but he

chil - dren say   he could,   laugh and   play just the   same   as   you   and
waved good - bye say - in', "Don't you   cry, I'll be   back   a - gain some

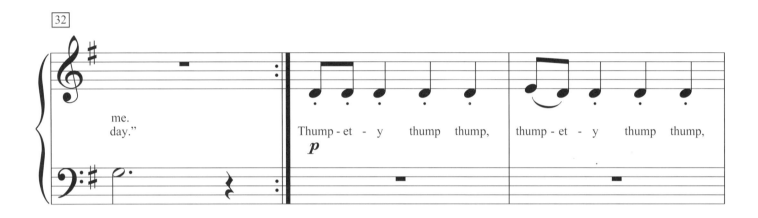

me.
day."   Thump - et - y   thump thump,   thump - et - y   thump thump,
                                    p

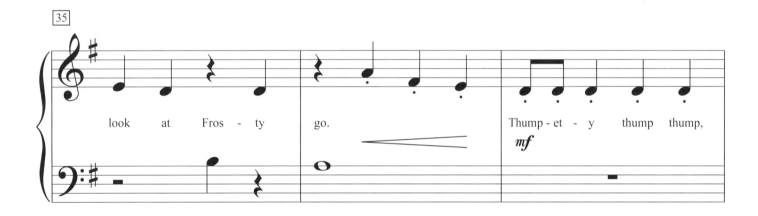

look   at   Fros - ty   go.   Thump - et - y   thump thump,
                                                               mf

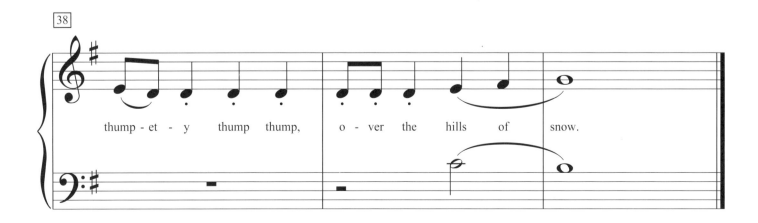

thump - et - y   thump thump,   o - ver the hills of   snow.

GOD BLESS US EVERYONE

from A CHRISTMAS CAROL

Words and Music by ALAN SILVESTRI
and GLEN BALLARD
Arranged by Phillip Keveren

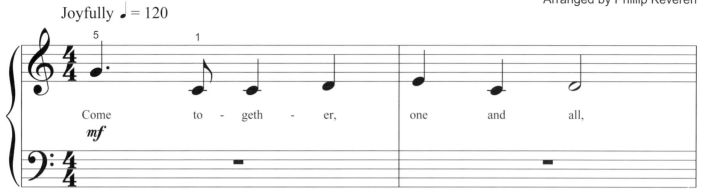

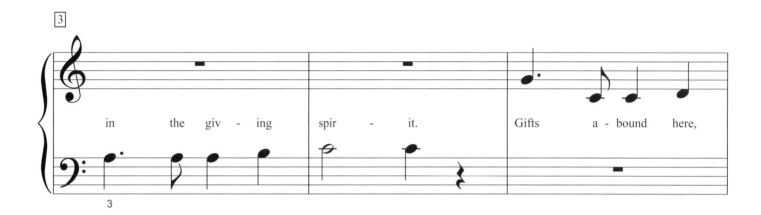

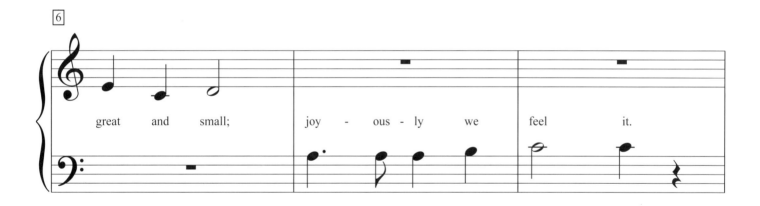

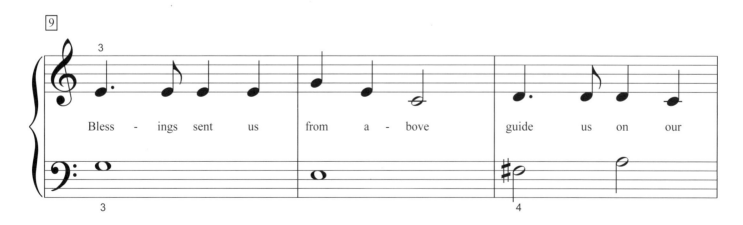

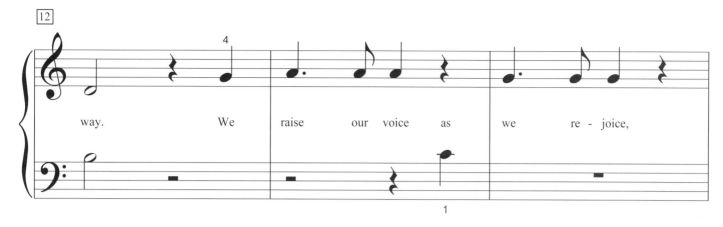

way.   We   raise   our   voice   as   we   re - joice,

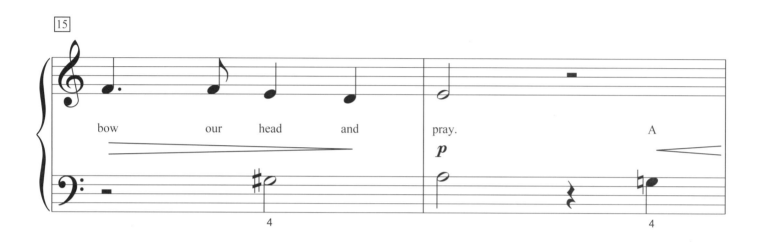

bow   our   head   and   pray.   A

p

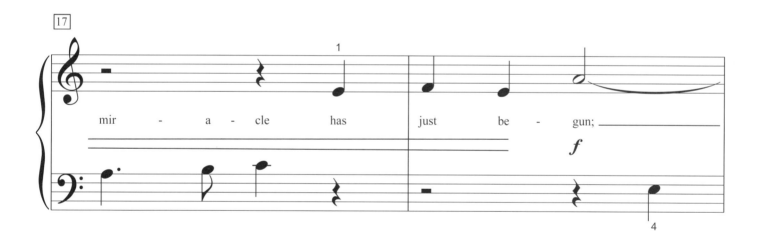

mir   -   a   -   cle   has   just   be   -   gun; _____

f

_____   God   bless   us   ev - 'ry - one.

JINGLE BELL ROCK

Words and Music by JOE BEAL
and JIM BOOTHE
Arranged by Phillip Keveren

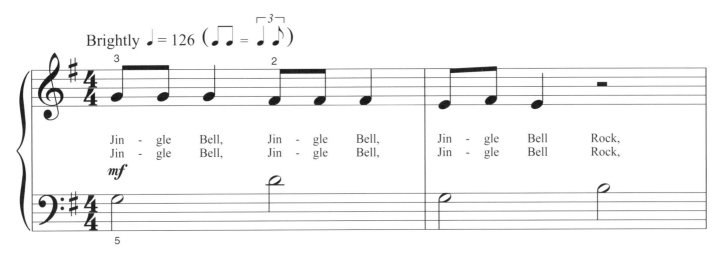

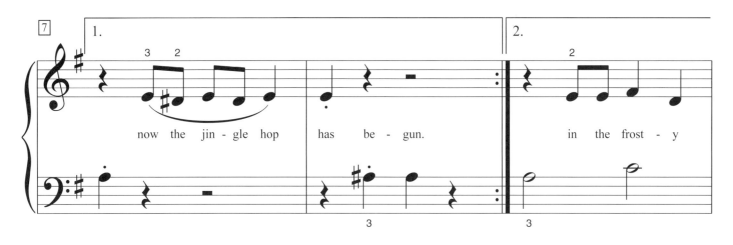

now the jin - gle hop has be - gun. | in the frost - y

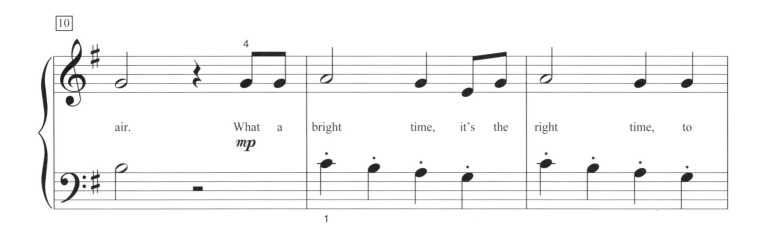

air. What a bright time, it's the right time, to

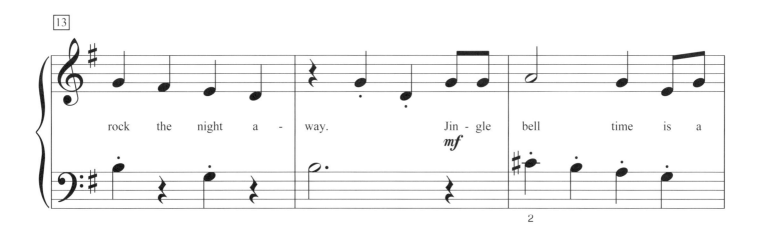

rock the night a - way. Jin - gle bell time is a

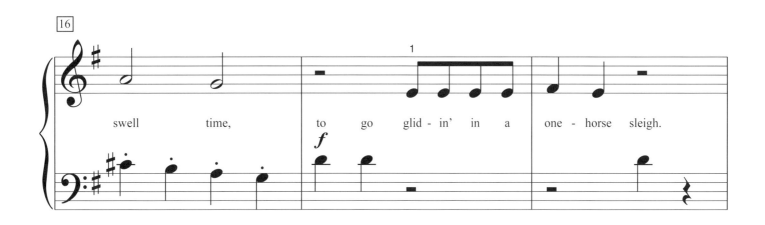

swell time, to go glid - in' in a one - horse sleigh.

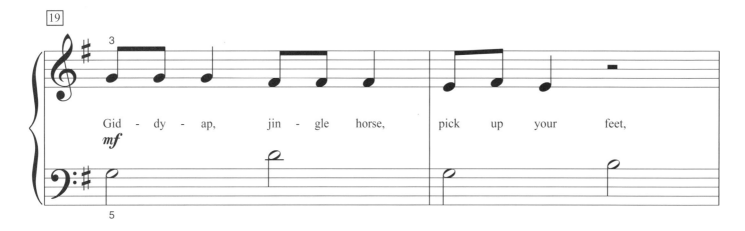

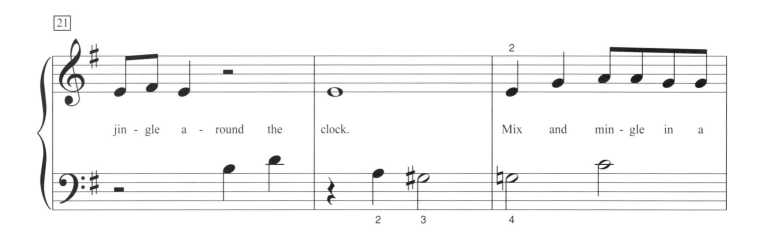

HOT CHOCOLATE
from Warner Bros. Pictures' THE POLAR EXPRESS

Words and Music by GLEN BALLARD
and ALAN SILVESTRI
Arranged by Phillip Keveren

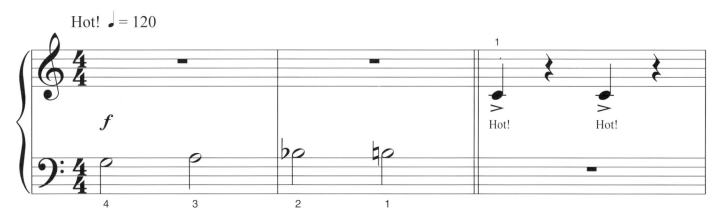

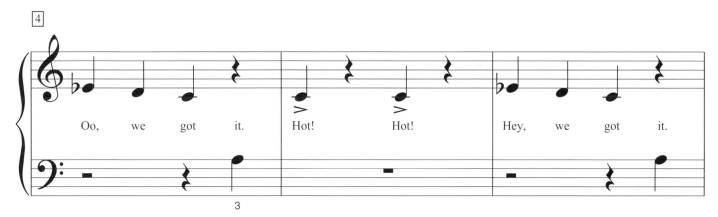

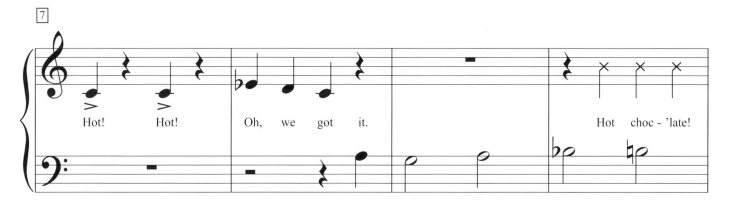

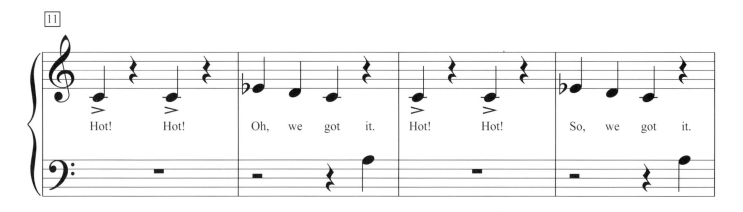

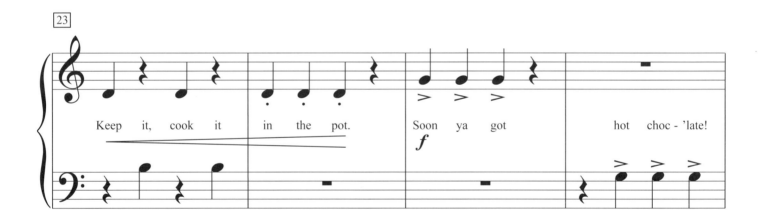

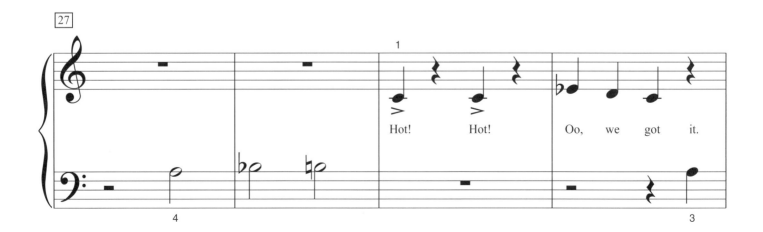

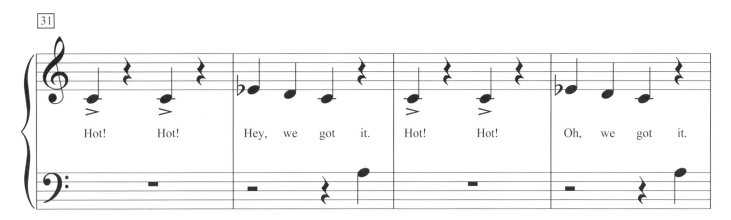

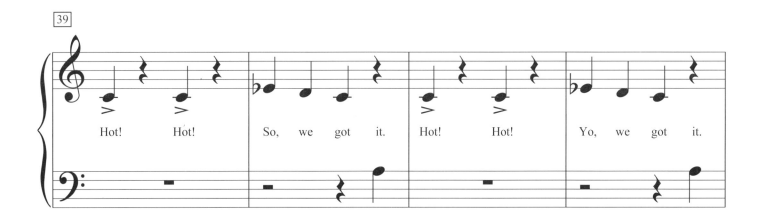

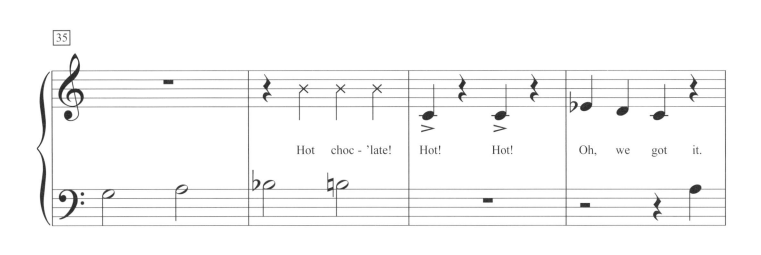

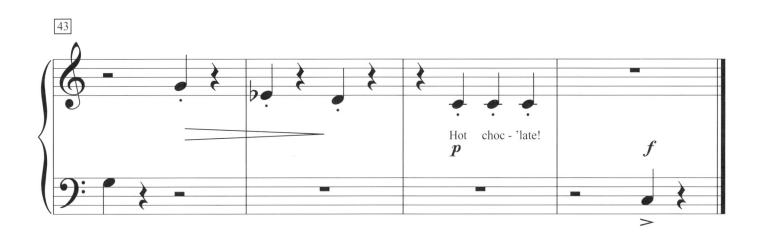

LITTLE SAINT NICK

Words and Music by BRIAN WILSON
and MIKE LOVE
Arranged by Phillip Keveren

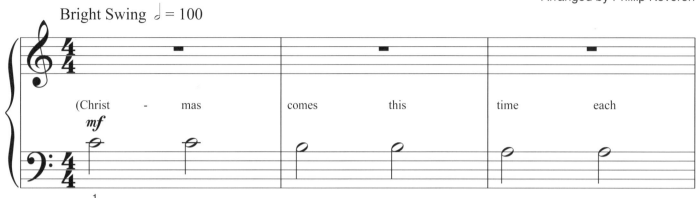

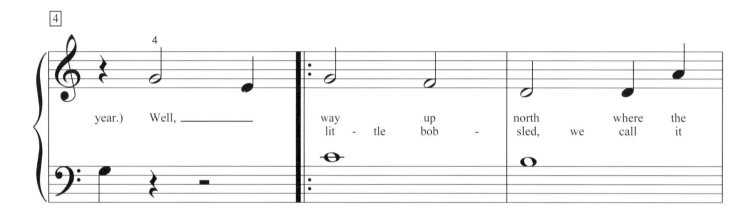

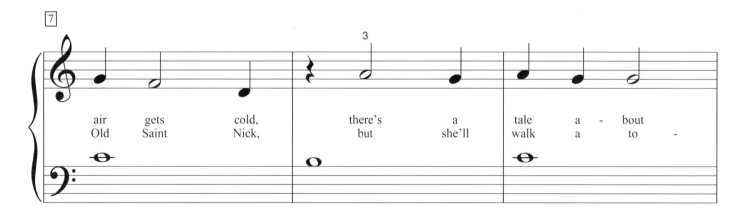

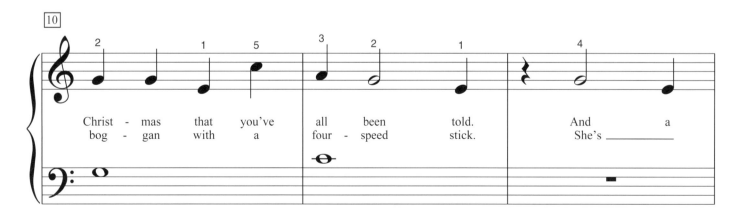

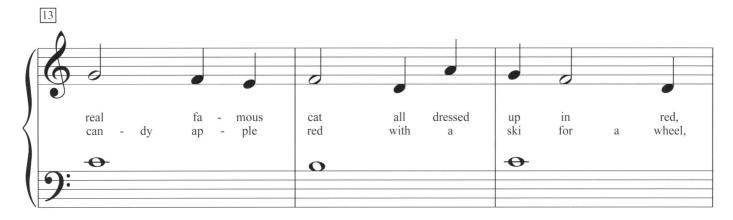

real   fa - mous   cat   all   dressed   up   in   red,
can - dy   ap - ple   red   with a   ski   for   a   wheel,

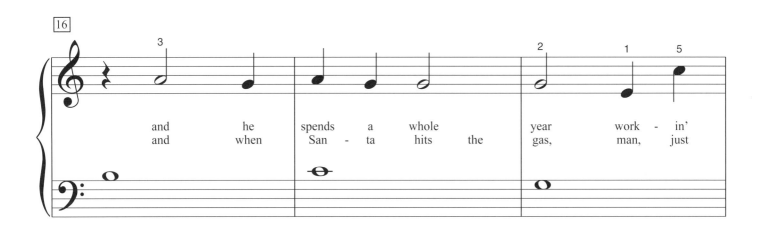

and   he   spends San - ta whole   year   work - in'
and   when   hits the   gas,   man,   just

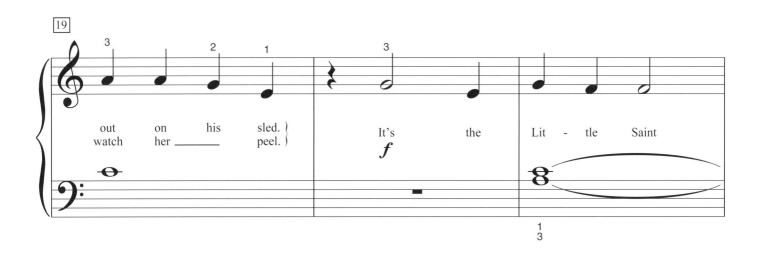

out   on   his   sled.   It's   the   Lit - tle   Saint
watch   her   peel.
f

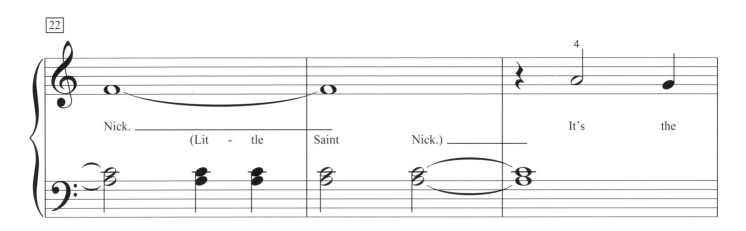

Nick.   (Lit - tle   Saint   Nick.)   It's   the

28

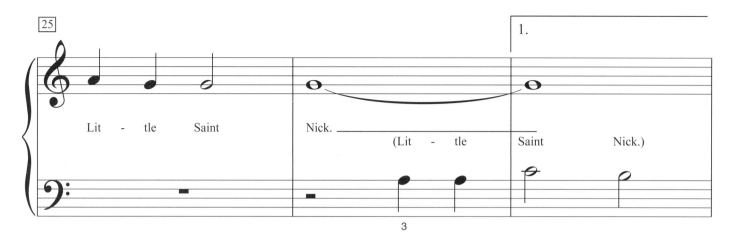

Lit - tle Saint Nick. _____ (Lit - tle Saint Nick.)

3

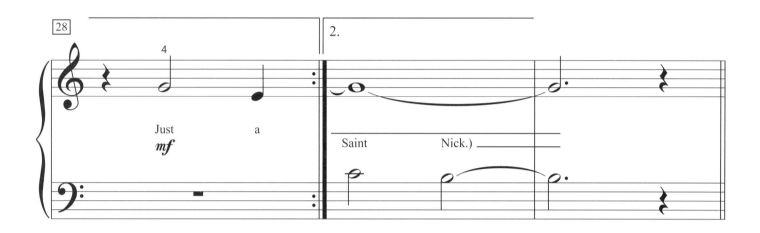

Just a

mf

Saint Nick.) _____

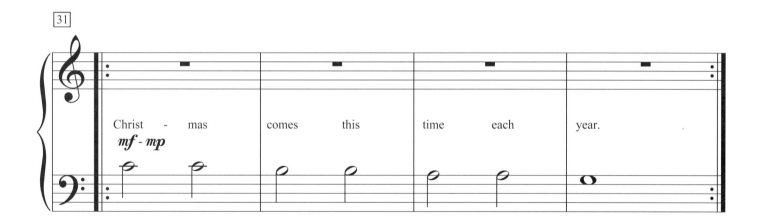

Christ - mas comes this time each year.

mf - mp

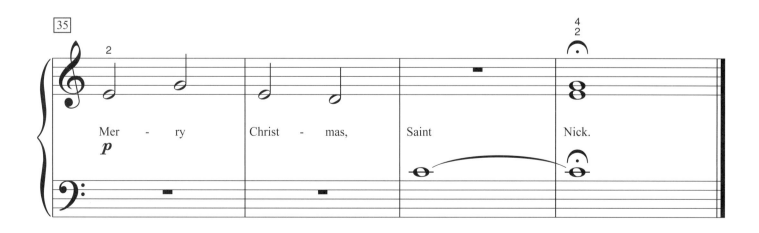

Mer - ry Christ - mas, Saint Nick.

p

MY FAVORITE THINGS

from THE SOUND OF MUSIC

Lyrics by OSCAR HAMMERSTEIN II
Music by RICHARD RODGERS
Arranged by Phillip Keveren

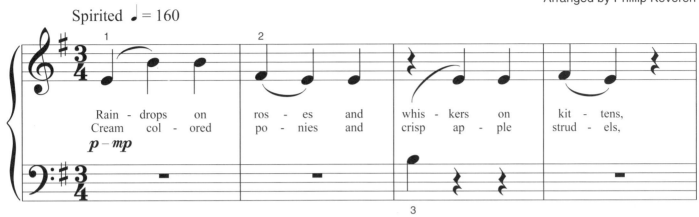

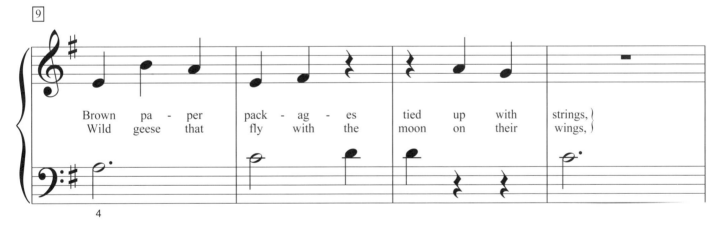

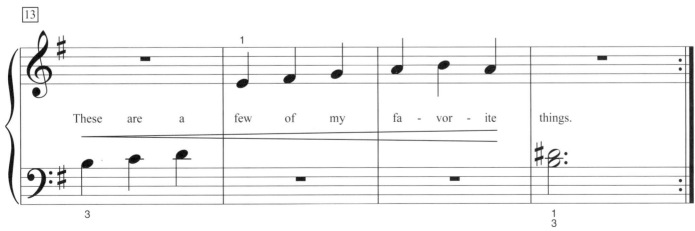

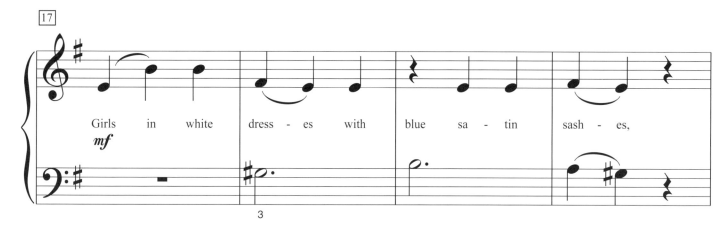

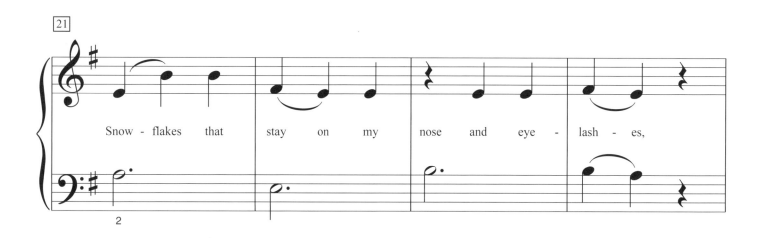

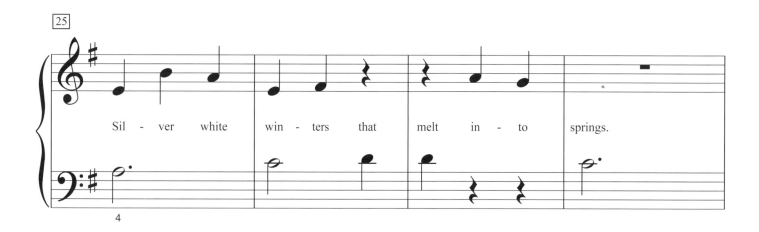

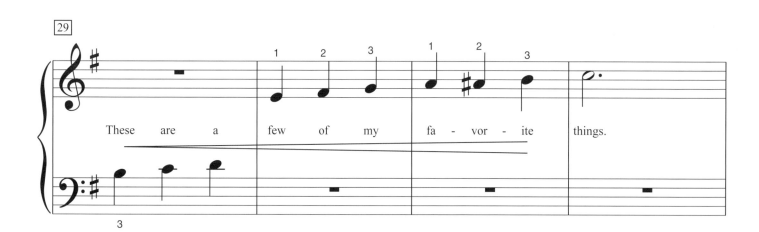

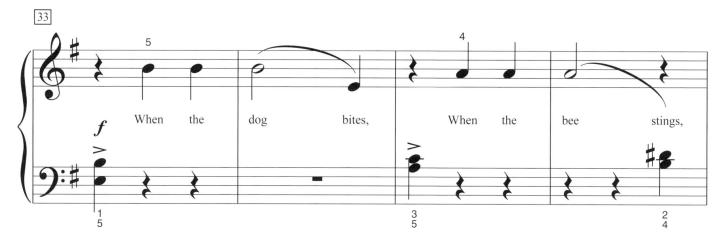

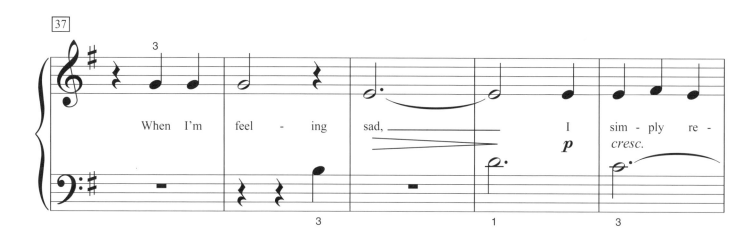

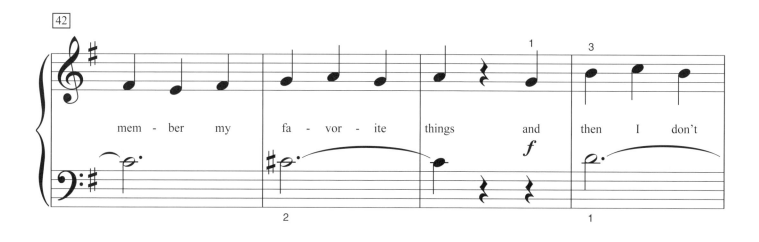

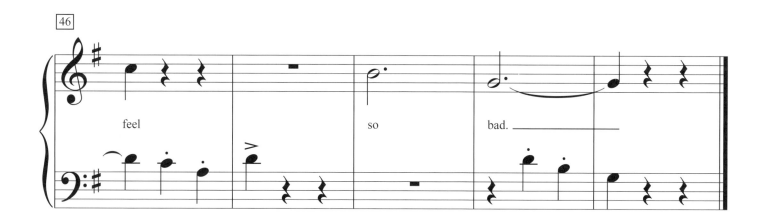

SILVER BELLS

from the Paramount Picture THE LEMON DROP KID

Words and Music by JAY LIVINGSTON
and RAY EVANS
Arranged by Phillip Keveren

Moderate Waltz ♩ = 120

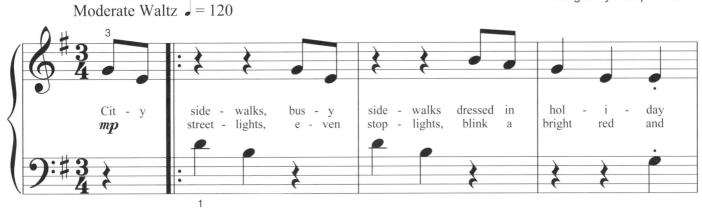

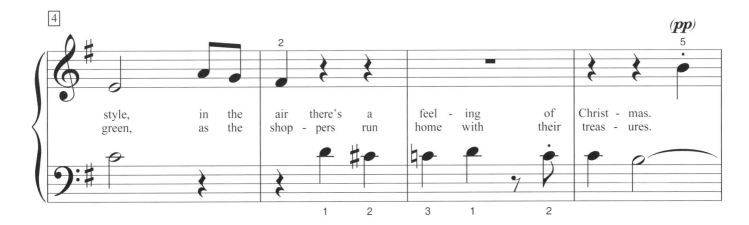

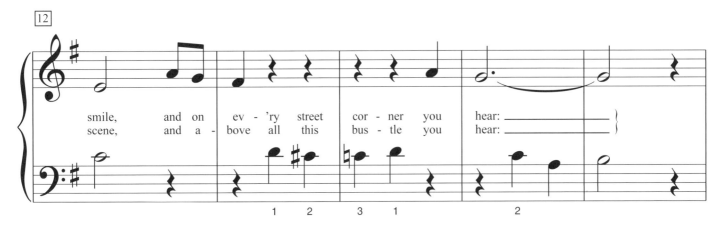

Sil - ver bells, _____ sil - ver bells, _____ it's Christ - mas

time in the cit - y. Ring - a - ling, _____

_____ hear them ring, _____ soon it will

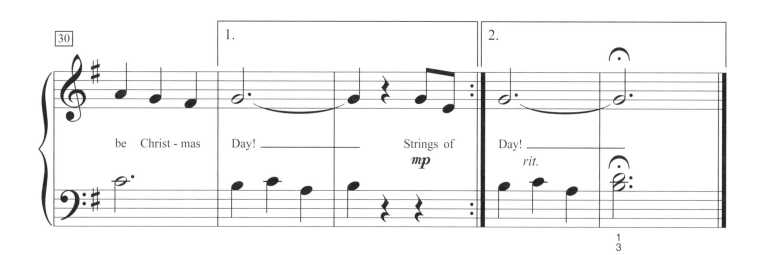

be Christ - mas Day! _____ Strings of Day! _____

SISTERS
from the Motion Picture Irving Berlin's WHITE CHRISTMAS

Words and Music by
IRVING BERLIN
Arranged by Phillip Keveren

Cheery, with a lilt ♩ = 116

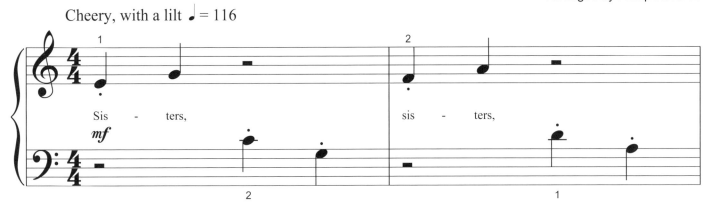

Sis - ters,   sis - ters,

there were nev - er such de - vot - ed sis - ters.

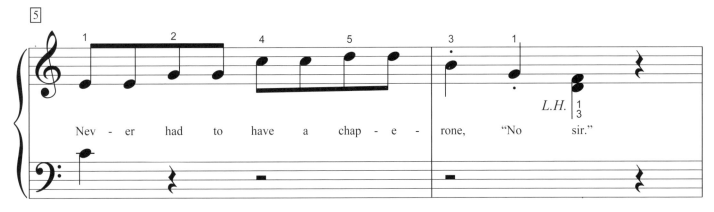

Nev - er had to have a chap - e - rone, "No sir."

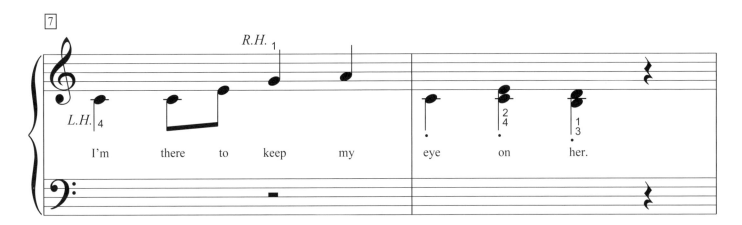

I'm there to keep my eye on her.

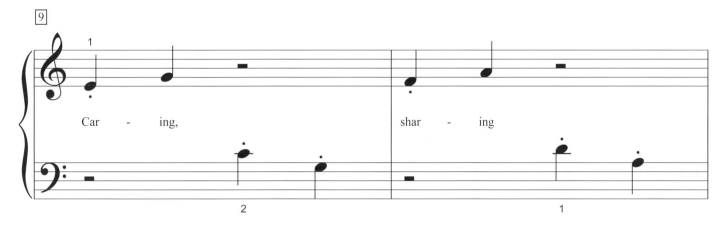

Car - ing, shar - ing

ev - 'ry lit - tle thing that we are wear - ing.

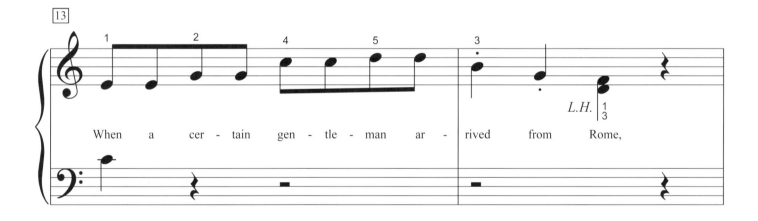

When a cer - tain gen - tle - man ar - rived from Rome,

L.H.

she wore the dress and I stayed home.

SOMEWHERE IN MY MEMORY

from the Twentieth Century Fox Motion Picture HOME ALONE

Words by LESLIE BRICUSSE
Music by JOHN WILLIAMS
Arranged by Phillip Keveren

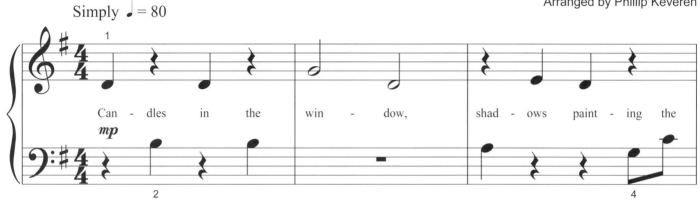

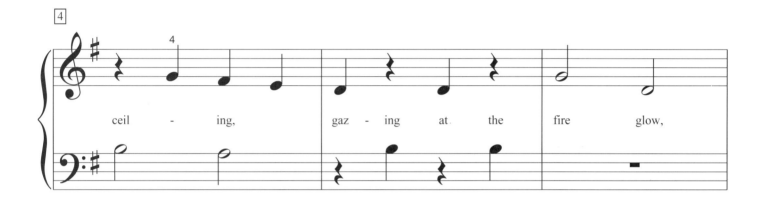

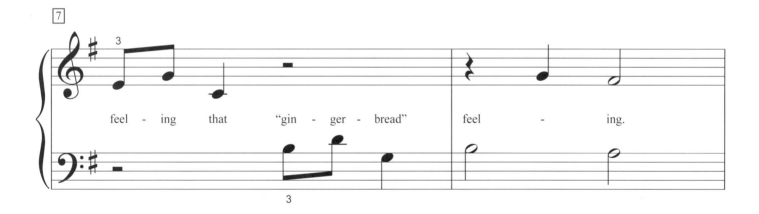

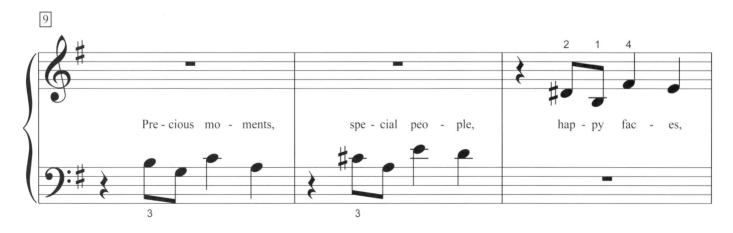

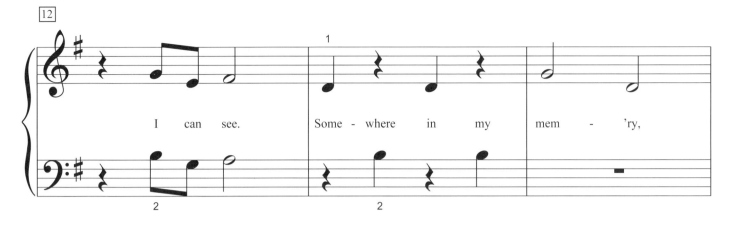

I can see. Some - where in my mem - 'ry,

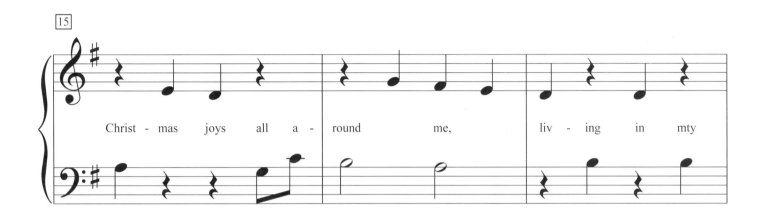

Christ - mas joys all a - round me, liv - ing in mty

mem - 'ry. All of the mu - sic, all of the mag - ic,

p

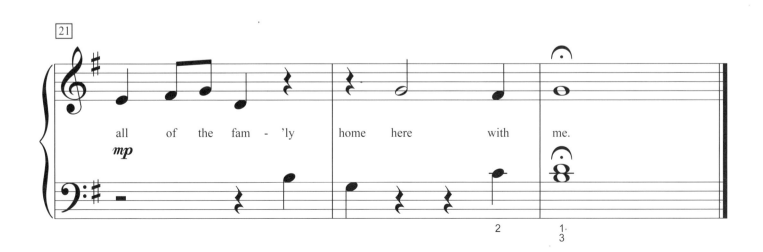

all of the fam - 'ly home here with me.

mp

WHERE ARE YOU CHRISTMAS?

from DR. SEUSS' HOW THE GRINCH STOLE CHRISTMAS

Words and Music by WILL JENNINGS,
JAMES HORNER and MARIAH CAREY
Arranged by Phillip Keveren

Gently ♩ = 60

mp Where are you, Christ - mas? Why can't I

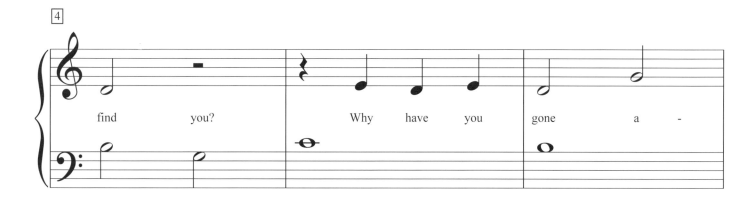

find you? Why have you gone a -

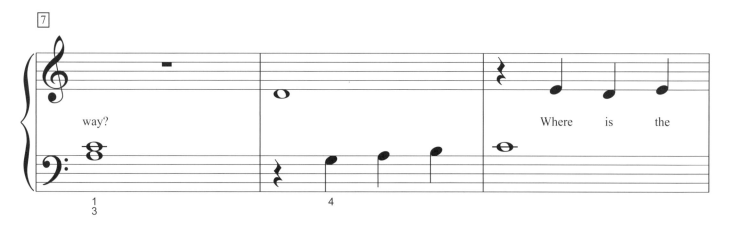

way? Where is the

laugh - ter you used to bring me?

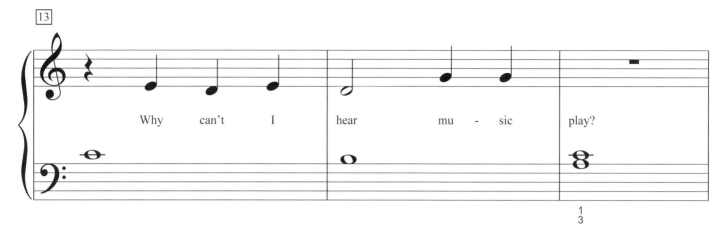

Why can't I hear mu - sic play?

My world is chang - ing.

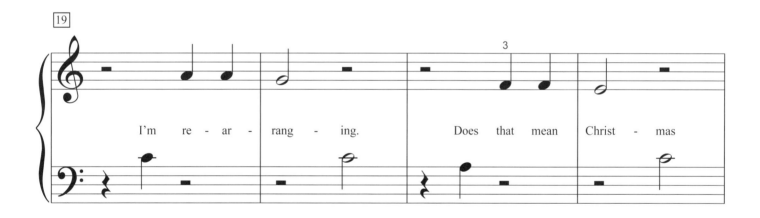

I'm re - ar - rang - ing. Does that mean Christ - mas

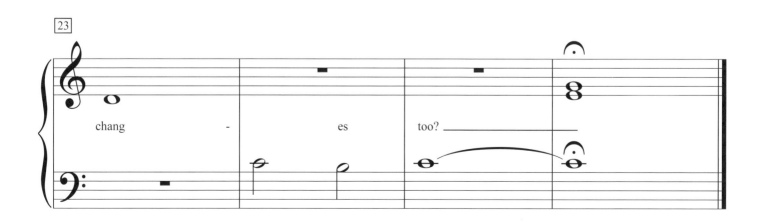

chang - es too? _____

SANTA CLAUS IS COMIN' TO TOWN

Words by HAVEN GILLESPIE
Music by J. FRED COOTS
Arranged by Phillip Keveren

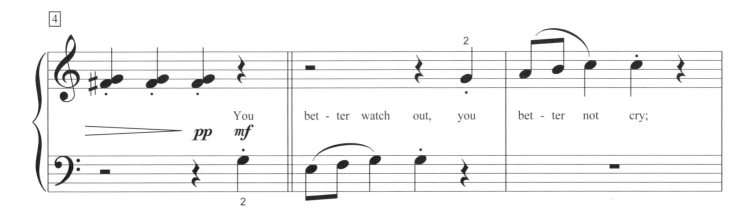

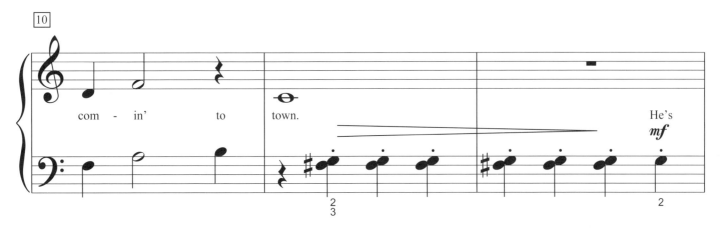

mak - ing a list and check - ing it twice, gon - na find out who's

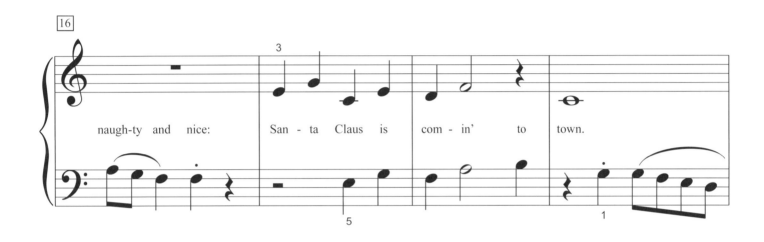

naugh-ty and nice: San - ta Claus is com - in' to town.

He sees you when you're sleep - in', he knows when you're a -

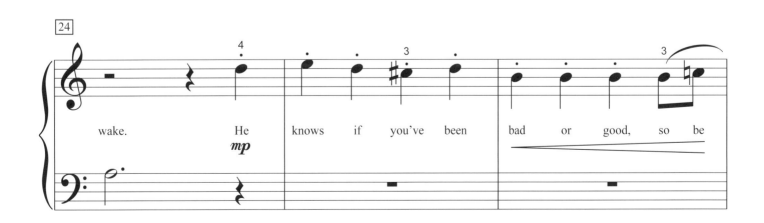

wake. He knows if you've been bad or good, so be

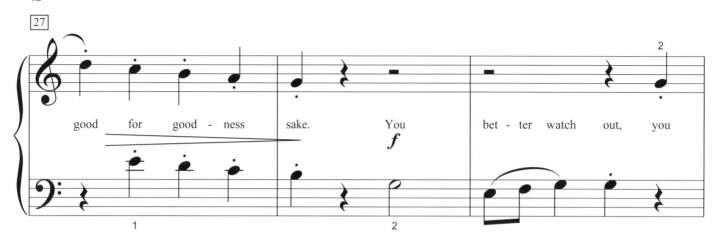

good for good - ness sake. You bet - ter watch out, you

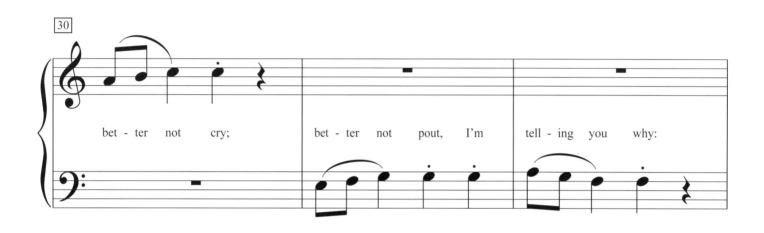

bet - ter not cry; bet - ter not pout, I'm tell - ing you why:

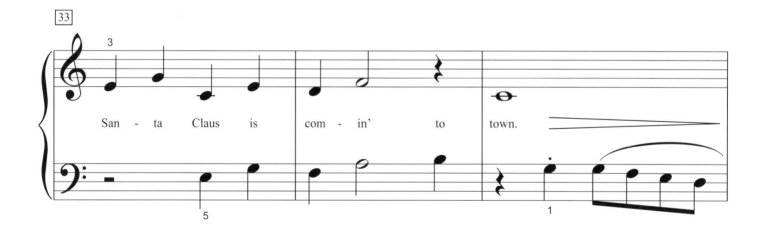

San - ta Claus is com - in' to town.

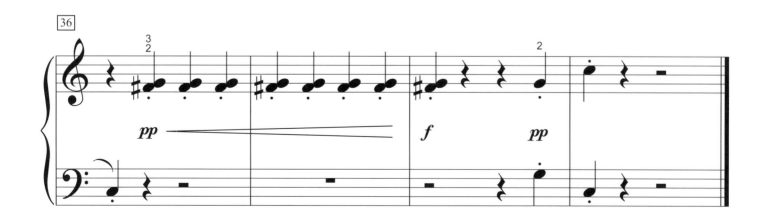

THE PHILLIP KEVEREN SERIES

FOLK SONG COLLECTIONS
FOR PIANO

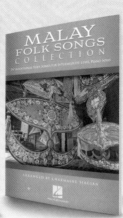

Introduce piano students to the music of world cultures with these folk songs arranged for intermediate piano solo. Each collection features 24 folk songs and includes detailed notes about the folk songs, beautiful illustrations, as well as a map of the regions.

AFRICAN AMERICAN FOLK SONGS COLLECTION

24 TRADITIONAL FOLK SONGS FOR
INTERMEDIATE LEVEL PIANO SOLO | *arr. Artina McCain*

The Bamboula • By and By • Deep River • Didn't My Lord Deliver Daniel? • Don't You Let Nobody Turn You Around • Every Time I Feel the Spirit • Give Me That Old Time Religion • Guide My Feet • I Want Jesus to Walk With Me • I Was Way Down A-Yonder • I'm a Soldier, Let Me Ride • In Bright Mansions Above • Lift Ev'ry Voice and Sing • Little David, Play on Your Harp • My Lord, What a Morning • Ride On, King Jesus • Run Mary Run • Sometimes I Feel Like a Motherless Child • Song of Conquest • Take Nabandji • Wade in the Water • Warriors' Song • Watch and Pray • What a Beautiful City.
00358084 Piano Solo...$12.99

IRISH FOLK SONGS COLLECTION

24 TRADITIONAL FOLK SONGS FOR
INTERMEDIATE LEVEL PIANO SOLO | *arr. June Armstrong*

As I Walked Out One Morning • Ballinderry • Blind Mary • Bunclody • Carrickfergus • The Castle of Dromore (The October Winds) • The Cliffs of Doneen • The Coolin • Courtin' in the Kitchen • Down Among the Ditches O • Down by the Salley Gardens • The Fairy Woman of Lough Leane • Follow Me Up to Carlow • The Gartan Mother's Lullaby • Huish the Cat • I'll Tell My Ma • Kitty of Coleraine • The Londonderry Air • My Lagan Love • My Love Is an Arbutus • Rocky Road to Dublin • Slieve Gallion Braes • Squire Parsons • That Night in Bethlehem.
00234359 Piano Solo...$9.99

MALAY FOLK SONGS COLLECTION

24 TRADITIONAL SONGS ARRANGED FOR
INTERMEDIATE LEVEL PIANO SOLO | *arr. Charmaine Siagian*

At Dawn • Chan Mali Chan • C'mon, Mama! • The Cockatoo • The Curvy Water Spinach Stalk • Five Little Chicks • God Bless the Sultan • The Goodbye Song • Great Indonesia • It's All Good Here • The Jumping Frog • Longing • Mak Inang • Milk Coffee • The Moon Kite • Morning Tide • My Country • Onward Singapore • Ponyfish • Song for the Ladybugs • The Stork Song • Suriram • Trek Tek Tek • Voyage of the Sampan.
00288420 Piano Solo...$10.99

CHINESE FOLK SONGS COLLECTION

24 TRADITIONAL SONGS ARRANGED FOR
INTERMEDIATE LEVEL PIANO SOLO | *arr. Joseph Johnson*

Beating the Wild Hog • Blue Flower • Carrying Song • Crescent Moon • Darkening Sky • Digging for Potatoes • Girl's Lament • Great Wall • Hand Drum Song • Homesick • Jasmine Flower Song • Little Cowherd • Love Song of the Prarie • Memorial • Mountaintop View • Northwest Rains • Running Horse Mountain • Sad, Rainy Day • Song of the Clown • The Sun Came Up Happy • Wa-Ha-Ha • Wedding Veil • White Flower • Woven Basket.
00296764 Piano Solo..$10.99

KOREAN FOLK SONGS COLLECTION

24 TRADITIONAL FOLK SONGS FOR
INTERMEDIATE LEVEL PIANO SOLO | *arr. Lawrence Lee*

Arirang • Autumn in the City • Birdie, Birdie • Boat Song • Catch the Tail • Chestnut • Cricket • Dance in the Moonlight • Five Hundred Years • Flowers • Fun Is Here • The Gate • Han River • Harvest • Jindo Field Song • Lullaby • The Mill • The Palace • The Pier • Three-Way Junction • Waterfall • Wild Herbs • Yearning • You and I.
00296810 Piano Solo..$10.99

JAPANESE FOLK SONGS COLLECTION

24 TRADITIONAL FOLK SONGS FOR
INTERMEDIATE LEVEL PIANO SOLO | *arr. Mika Goto*

Blooming Flowers • Come Here, Fireflies • Counting Game • The Fisherman's Song • Going to the Shrine • Harvest Song • Itsuki Lullaby • Joyful Doll Festival • Kimigayo • Let's Sing • My Hometown • Picking Tea Leaves • The Rabbit on the Moon • Rain • Rain Showers • Rock-Paper-Scissors • Sakura • Seven Baby Crows • Takeda Lullaby • Time to Go Home • Village Festival • Where Are You From? • Wish I Could Go • You're It!
00296891 Piano Solo..$9.99

halleonard.com

0721
067
Prices, contents and availability subject to change without notice.

POPULAR SONGS
HAL LEONARD STUDENT PIANO LIBRARY

The **Hal Leonard Student Piano Library** has great songs, and you will find all your favorites here: Disney classics, Broadway and movie favorites, and today's top hits. These graded collections are skillfully and imaginatively arranged for students and pianists at every level, from elementary solos with teacher accompaniments to sophisticated piano solos for the advancing pianist.

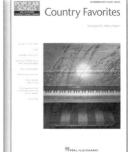

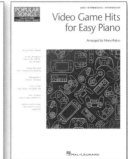

Adele
arr. Mona Rejino
Correlates with HLSPL Level 5
00159590...............................$12.99

The Beatles
arr. Eugénie Rocherolle
Correlates with HLSPL Level 5
00296649...............................$12.99

Irving Berlin Piano Duos
arr. Don Heitler and Jim Lyke
Correlates with HLSPL Level 5
00296838...............................$14.99

Broadway Favorites
arr. Phillip Keveren
Correlates with HLSPL Level 4
00279192...............................$12.99

Chart Hits
arr. Mona Rejino
Correlates with HLSPL Level 5
00296710...............................$8.99

Christmas at the Piano
arr. Lynda Lybeck-Robinson
Correlates with HLSPL Level 4
00298194...............................$12.99

Christmas Cheer
arr. Phillip Keveren
Correlates with HLSPL Level 4
00296616...............................$8.99

Classic Christmas Favorites
arr. Jennifer & Mike Watts
Correlates with HLSPL Level 5
00129582...............................$9.99

Christmas Time Is Here
arr. Eugénie Rocherolle
Correlates with HLSPL Level 5
00296614...............................$8.99

Classic Joplin Rags
arr. Fred Kern
Correlates with HLSPL Level 5
00296743...............................$9.99

Classical Pop – Lady Gaga Fugue & Other Pop Hits
arr. Giovanni Dettori
Correlates with HLSPL Level 5
00296921...............................$12.99

Contemporary Movie Hits
arr. by Carol Klose, Jennifer Linn and Wendy Stevens
Correlates with HLSPL Level 5
00296780...............................$8.99

Contemporary Pop Hits
arr. Wendy Stevens
Correlates with HLSPL Level 3
00296836...............................$8.99

Cool Pop
arr. Mona Rejino
Correlates with HLSPL Level 5
00360103...............................$12.99

Country Favorites
arr. Mona Rejino
Correlates with HLSPL Level 5
00296861...............................$9.99

Disney Favorites
arr. Phillip Keveren
Correlates with HLSPL Levels 3/4
00296647...............................$10.99

Disney Film Favorites
arr. Mona Rejino
Correlates with HLSPL Level 5
00296809 ....$10.99

Disney Piano Duets
arr. Jennifer & Mike Watts
Correlates with HLSPL Level 5
00113759...............................$13.99

Double Agent! Piano Duets
arr. Jeremy Siskind
Correlates with HLSPL Level 5
00121595...............................$12.99

Easy Christmas Duets
arr. Mona Rejino & Phillip Keveren
Correlates with HLSPL Levels 3/4
00237139...............................$9.99

Easy Disney Duets
arr. Jennifer and Mike Watts
Correlates with HLSPL Level 4
00243727...............................$12.99

Four Hands on Broadway
arr. Fred Kern
Correlates with HLSPL Level 5
00146177...............................$12.99

Frozen Piano Duets
arr. Mona Rejino
Correlates with HLSPL Levels 3/4
00144294...............................$12.99

Hip-Hop for Piano Solo
arr. Logan Evan Thomas
Correlates with HLSPL Level 5
00360950...............................$12.99

Jazz Hits for Piano Duet
arr. Jeremy Siskind
Correlates with HLSPL Level 5
00143248...............................$12.99

Elton John
arr. Carol Klose
Correlates with HLSPL Level 5
00296721...............................$10.99

Joplin Ragtime Duets
arr. Fred Kern
Correlates with HLSPL Level 5
00296771...............................$8.99

Movie Blockbusters
arr. Mona Rejino
Correlates with HLSPL Level 5
00232850...............................$10.99

The Nutcracker Suite
arr. Lynda Lybeck-Robinson
Correlates with HLSPL Levels 3/4
00147906...............................$8.99

Pop Hits for Piano Duet
arr. Jeremy Siskind
Correlates with HLSPL Level 5
00224734...............................$12.99

Sing to the King
arr. Phillip Keveren
Correlates with HLSPL Level 5
00296808...............................$8.99

Smash Hits
arr. Mona Rejino
Correlates with HLSPL Level 5
00284841...............................$10.99

Spooky Halloween Tunes
arr. Fred Kern
Correlates with HLSPL Levels 3/4
00121550...............................$9.99

Today's Hits
arr. Mona Rejino
Correlates with HLSPL Level 5
00296646...............................$9.99

Top Hits
arr. Jennifer and Mike Watts
Correlates with HLSPL Level 5
00296894...............................$10.99

Top Piano Ballads
arr. Jennifer Watts
Correlates with HLSPL Level 5
00197926...............................$10.99

Video Game Hits
arr. Mona Rejino
Correlates with HLSPL Level 4
00300310...............................$12.99

You Raise Me Up
arr. Deborah Brady
Correlates with HLSPL Level 2/3
00296576...............................$7.95

HAL•LEONARD®
7777 W. BLUEMOUND RD. P.O. BOX 13819 MILWAUKEE, WI 53213

Prices, contents and availability subject to change without notice. Prices may vary outside the U.S.

Visit our website at **www.halleonard.com**

BEGINNING PIANO SOLO

Hal Leonard Beginning Piano Solos are created for students in the first and second years of study. These arrangements include a simple presentation of melody and harmony for a first "solo" experience. Go to halleonard.com for song lists.

Adele
00156395 10 songs.................... $15.99

The Beatles
00306568 8 songs.................... $14.99

Songs of the Beatles
00307153 8 songs.................... $10.99

Beethoven
00338054 10 songs.................... $9.99

Broadway Favorites
00319408 10 songs.................... $9.99

Cartoon Favorites
00279152 10 songs.................... $9.99

A Charlie Brown Christmas
00311767 10 songs.................... $12.99

Charlie Brown Favorites
00153652 12 songs.................... $10.99

Chart Hits
00362594 10 songs.................... $12.99

Christmastime
00101873 8 songs.................... $9.99

Classical Favorites
00311063 8 songs.................... $8.99

Contemporary Disney Solos
00316082 10 songs.................... $14.99

Disney Classics
00311431 9 songs.................... $10.99

Disney Favorites
00334221 10 songs.................... $12.99

Disney Hits
00264691 10 songs.................... $10.99

Billie Eilish
00362598 10 songs.................... $14.99

First Book of Disney Solos
00316058 8 songs.................... $12.99

Frozen
00130375 7 songs.................... $14.99

Frozen 2
00329567 8 songs.................... $14.99

Gospel Hymn Favorites
00311799 10 songs.................... $9.99

Great TV Themes
00319409 10 songs.................... $9.99

Greatest Pop Hits
00311064 8 songs.................... $9.95

Happy Songs
00346762 10 songs.................... $10.99

Hit Movie Songs
00338186 10 songs.................... $9.99

It's a Beautiful Day with Mister Rogers
00319418 7 songs.................... $8.99

Jazz Standards
00311065 8 songs.................... $9.95

Best of Carole King
00118420 8 songs.................... $10.99

Les Misérables
00103351 9 songs.................... $14.99

The Lion King
00319465 9 songs.................... $12.99

The Most Beautiful Songs Ever
00110402 50 songs.................... $14.99

The Phantom of the Opera
00103239 9 songs.................... $14.99

Pop Hits
00175142 10 songs.................... $10.99

Praise & Worship Favorites
00311271 8 songs.................... $9.95

The Sound of Music
00316037 10 songs.................... $10.99

Star Wars
00110287 10 songs.................... $14.99

Best of Taylor Swift
00175650 10 songs.................... $12.99

10 Fun Favorites
00110390 10 songs.................... $9.99

Top Hits of 2016
00194558 10 songs.................... $9.99

Wicked
00109365 8 songs.................... $14.99

John Williams
00194545 14 songs.................... $11.99

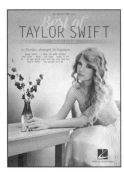
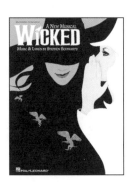

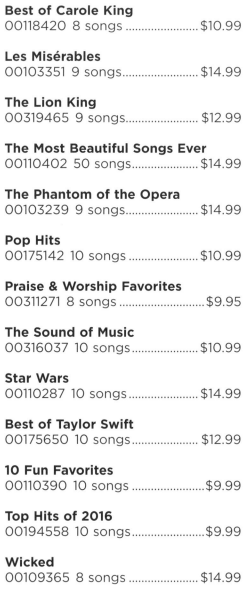

HAL•LEONARD®

Order these and many more songbooks from your favorite music retailer at
halleonard.com